Decentralization at the Grass Roots: Political Innovation in New York City & London

H. V. SAVITCH
New York University

and

MADELEINE ADLER
Queens College

 SAGE PUBLICATIONS / Beverly Hills / London

For information address:

SAGE PUBLICATIONS, INC.
275 South Beverly Drive
Beverly Hills, California 90212

SAGE PUBLICATIONS LTD
St George's House / 44 Hatton Garden
London EC1N 8ER

International Standard Book Number 0-8039-0453-3

Library of Congress Catalog Card No. 74-76489

FIRST PRINTING

When citing a professional paper, please use the proper form. Remember to cite the
correct Sage Professional Paper series title and include the paper number. One of the
two following formats can be adapted (depending on the style manual used):

(1) OSTROM, E. et al. (1973) "Community Organization and the Provision of Police
Services." Sage Professional Papers in Administrative and Policy Studies, 1, 03-001.
Beverly Hills and London: Sage Pubns.

OR

(2) Ostrom, Elinor, et al. 1973 *Community Organization and the Provision of Police
Services.* Sage Professional Papers in Administrative and Policy Studies, vol. 1, series
no. 03-001. Beverly Hills and London: Sage Publications.

CONTENTS

Decentralization at the Grass Roots: Political Innovation in New York City & London

H. V. SAVITCH
New York University
   and

MADELEINE ADLER
Queens College

I. INTRODUCTION

Decentralization is among the more recent words in our political lexicon that arouse strong prejudices. For some it is a new weapon through which ordinary citizens can regain control of their communities and renew their cities; for others it is seen as a ruse which detracts from the city's present problems and resurrects old ones (Altshuler, 1970; Kotler, 1969; Fantini et al., 1970; Kaufman, 1969; Kristol, 1968). Scholars question the meaning of decentralization and proceed to explicate its definitions. There are, of course, many conceptions of decentralization but the term can broadly be defined as "bringing government closer to the people" (Nordlinger, 1972: 5). This may be accomplished in two ways. First, government can be brought closer to the citizenry by providing for increased policy inputs, which is political decentralization. This entails setting up channels for citizen participation in basic decisions relating to finances, planning, and personnel. Second, local government might be administratively decentralized, allowing local offices to be physically reorganized so that constituents can have better access to civil servants (Nordlinger, 1972: 6). The latter form of decentralization usually amounts to a deconcentration of administrative authority by spreading offices throughout the communities which are served. The two forms of decentralization are not mutually

AUTHOR'S NOTE: *The authors are grateful to their colleagues in the Department of Politics at New York University and Queens College respectively for their scholarly contributions to this research. Professor Savitch is grateful to the National Science Foundation Institutional Grants Award and the New York University Arts and* exclusive and can be mixed in a variety of ways. The decentralized areas selected for this study represent, in fact, hybrids of political and administrative decentralization and we have paid attention to the inextricability of the two forms.

Aside from the many nuances decentralization can take, much of the debate on the subject has been carried on a hypothetical plane and remains there (Arnstein, 1969; Altshuler, 1970; Felser, 1965: 536-566; Lipsky, 1971: 391-410; Schmandt, 1973).

When research goes beyond conjecture it is too often on very narrow ground. Studies of model cities, community corporations, and educational experiments are useful but idiosyncratic. These experiments are limited to isolated problems—housing, economic development, education—which labor under extraordinary conditions of poverty, social breakdown, and urban wreckage. Whatever one might think of our cities, the slum is not its microcosm (Berube and Gittell, 1969; Brower, 1970; Miller and Rein, 1969: 15-25; Rosenbloom and Morris, 1969). If anything, considerable differences emerge when comparing efforts at urban decentralization. Much of this is attributable to the contrasting conditions under which reorganizations have been initiated. In this study we have focused on both the political and administrative conditions of decentralization in two cities—New York and London. Seven decentralized areas—or subsystems—have been examined in both of these cities.[1] The essential question, we believe, is not whether decentralization is feasible or not; but why and how particular conditions promote decentralization while others hinder it?

By the word conditions, we mean the arrangements and circumstances under which decentralization has been initiated. The political and administrative aspects of these conditions deal with allocations of power for making and carrying out policy. In considering these arrangements, careful attention will be given to: the relative autonomy of each decentralized area; the political structures which have grown within each of them; and the interaction of leaders, bureaucrats, and groups which form the working parts of each subsystem.

It is our contention that much of the difficulty surrounding urban decentralization can be explained by examining how political and administrative conditions shape the relationships between participants within

Science Grant for the assistance given to him. His special thanks goes to the Greater London Group and particularly to Professor Wm. A. Robson of the London School of Economics and Political Science. Professor Adler is indebted to Professor Julius C. C. Edelstein, Dean of Urban Programs and Policy at City University of New York and Howard N. Mantel, Director of the Urban Analysis Center at the City University of New York for the grants which made her research possible.

decentralized networks. What comes out of these relationships is a capacity—or lack of capacity—to structure interaction so that it works to strengthen or weaken the subsystem. At one end of the continuum a healthy dynamic evolves which keeps leaders formulating policy, bureaucrats in tow administering it, and various groups overseeing it and making new demands for improvement. At the other end, a spiral of conflict and confusion ensues. Leaders are rendered helpless to initiate policy, bureaucrats becomes paralyzed by countervailing orders and groups engage in bitter controversy which cripples even the most modest innovation.

The seven decentralized subsystems used for this study consist of four in New York City and three in London. The New York operations, called "community districts," include identifiable neighborhoods in various parts of the city. These are Crown Heights and Bushwick in Brooklyn, Wakefield-Edenwald in the Bronx; and Washington Heights in Manhattan. The New York projects were begun in 1972, at the discretion of the Mayor, and represent the core of an experiment in administrative decentralization. In London, urban reorganization began in 1965, under an act of parliament. There, decentralization is part of a much broader reorganization plan, involving thirty-two London "boroughs" as the decentralized areas are called. The three boroughs selected for this study are Tower Hamlets, Islington, and Wandsworth.

Despite the cross-cultural differences, the London and New York experiences have some interesting parallels. In both cities the decentralized subsystems are not very different in size of population. New York's neighborhood districts, on the average, have populations of about 150,000, while the comparable average for each of the London boroughs is 200,000.[2]

Also, there are remarkable similarities in the social and urban character of the subsystems. This holds true for six of the seven areas, with Bushwick remaining the only glaring exception. All six, to use urban parlance, are "inner city" and "transitional" areas. That is, older neighborhoods which are neither slums nor desirable residential locations, but susceptible to tipping in either direction. Bushwick alone, or large portions of it, qualifies as a blighted neighborhood.

Because of their transitional nature, the quality of municipal services is vital to the future of each area and there is considerable strain on them. In New York and London, administrators see service improvement as a key task. Smoother traffic flows and easier parking are essential to building stable business districts. Recreational facilities and usable spaces encourage neighborhood stability—and so forth. Understandably, the areas in each city have their own priorities. Better housing is critical in London, while nothing consumes the community districts in New York as does public safety.

Almost all of the subsystems are predominantly working and lower middle class in composition. In Wakefield-Edenwald, Washington Heights, and Crown Heights there are large numbers of blue collar workers, municipal employees, clerks and semi-skilled laborers. For these three areas, annual per capita income falls in the range of three to four thousand dollars. Bushwick is a partial exception to the rule with per capita income of 1900 dollars. It alone has a large nonworking poor population. Many families are on welfare and unemployment is high (U.S. Bureau of the Census, 1970).

The London boroughs of Tower Hamlets, Islington and Wandsworth resemble their New York counterparts. Of these three, however, Tower Hamlets stands out, consisting of a heavy working class with marginal incomes. Many of these families lack proper toilet facilities, and it is necessary for the borough to maintain extensive public baths. Islington and Wandsworth are better off. Each are lower middle class in character, but have substantial numbers of professional and managerial people. Sections of Islington, in fact, have undergone a resurgence, where formerly overcrowded Georgian homes have been renovated by affluent home-owners (Greater London Council, Municipal Year Book, 1970: 885-6, 907-10).

The most significant parallel in both cities is administrative. Without exception all of the decentralized areas, which are composite entities, provide an array of municipal services, such as housing maintenance, public health, recreation and social services for the young and elderly. As composite entities, each of the decentralized areas are responsible for problem-solving which cuts across all aspects of the bureaucracy. As such, service intergration and coordination is a central concern. If streets are to be kept tidy; police, traffic, and sanitation men must work in conjunction to remove abandoned vehicles, enforce parking prohibitions during particular times, and sweep the streets clean.

In New York, the decentralization experiment was intended to integrate a number of services and transfer some decision-making authority to local agency chiefs within each of the four community districts. Eight municipal agencies representing some of the most critical services within the city participated. These services included: police, sanitation, parks, transportation, drug prevention, health, housing maintenance, and social services. Local representatives from each of the agencies performing these functions were to be organized into a Service Cabinet within each community which would meet monthly to identify problems, set priorities and offer solutions to the problems identified. A District Manager was also appointed to act as cabinet chairman, coordinate functions, and encourage local agency administrators to work together on common problems within a community.

In London, the problems may differ but the objectives are the same. A homeless family in need of help may require simultaneous attention from a social worker, a housing official, and a medical officer. An approach which treats this situation as a series of interrelated problems may be more efficient—and humane—than the best services provided in isolation from one another. London's thirty-two boroughs have far more reaching powers, but resemble New York's community districts in many ways. The boroughs are responsible for housing, public health, welfare and children's services, sanitation pickups, roads (other than main), libraries, local planning, and inspection services (Smallwood, 1965: 25). The carrying out of these responsibilities is under the direction of the Town Clerk/Chief Executive who is appointed by a popularly elected borough council. It is the chief executive who coordinates service departments and personnel to facilitate problem identification, planning and problem-solving.

Because all of these decentralized areas are supposed to operate as composite entities, responsibilities can be fixed on top echelon administrators. Neighborhood districts or boroughs can be evaluated as overall performers, with presumably better result through time. This is how decentralization works theoretically. Reality, in some cases, tells a different tale.

Some of the contrasting conditions underlying the New York and London experiences invite closer comparison than their similarities. The political and administrative aspects of these conditions, we claim, have operated to structure interaction between participants in each of the decentralized areas. In some cases interaction has produced results which strengthen the subsystems; in others it has weakened them.

This interaction may be analyzed by focusing on three concepts. Each of these concepts is designed to reveal different conditions within a decentralized area and are identified as: (1) subsystem legitimacy; (2) leadership capability; and (3) structural capability.

By subsystem legitimacy, we mean the degree to which each of the decentralized areas were accorded acceptance and recognition. Legitimacy, in this case, involves both legal and extralegal sources of support (Lipset, 1960: 64-79; Easton, 1965). Thus a decentralized area may be operating on the basis of statute, but may also have been initiated with a good deal of ceremony and fanfare; thereby boosting its initial recognition. Some subsystems may enjoy continued publicity from the media, or possess visible signs of recognition like impressive facilities or its own symbols. Others may have very little in the way of this "ongoing legitimacy" and its image may be faded, if not absent, within its own locale.

A second factor affecting subsystem legitimacy is the extent to which decentralization is the product of institutional action. Subsystems which are established through a lengthy process and ratified by some collective body (legislature, charter commission, referendum, etc.) are likely to be accepted as stable institutions. On the other hand, decentralized projects which are perceived as the handiwork of one man, or faction, will meet with less respect, if not resistance.

Still a third factor affecting legitimacy is the presence of competing institutions within the same area. A subsystem which holds a monopoly of political presence in a neighborhood will undoubtedly strengthen its acceptance—both within the neighborhood and vis-a-vis outsiders. Where there is more than one decentralized project, legitimacy will be diluted and so will the vitality of the subsystem.

The concept of leadership capability deals with the effectiveness with which top political or administrative officers guide the subsystem. This guidance involves a blending of direction, management, and manipulation of resources as well as people. Leaders who have considerable formal powers over budget, appointments, and policy are at a conspicuous advantage. The more levers a leader can pull with respect to funding his favorite causes, setting goals and selecting personnel, the greater his capability. There is no question that the availability of formal sanctions and inducements enhances this power and we shall keep this in mind.

But leadership capability also depends on intangible factors; the personality and skills that an executive brings to the job is crucial. A leader may have little in the way of formal power, yet be able to persuade other participants to use their resources to strengthen his role. He may begin with scanty prerogatives, yet pyramid them into larger discretionary authority; the way a clever investor parlays a small sum into a corporate empire.

A leader's identification of his role in a larger scheme is important to the subsystem. If he is able to act forcefully, as an innovator or temporizer, he sets one tone. The leader who adopts a less forceful role, as either an "implementer" or "go between," sets another mood (Dahl, 1961).

Nevertheless, a top executive does not determine his role by himself. Most often he is bound by the conditions and circumstances which affect his office. These conditions include the socio-economic characteristics of the subsystem in which he functions, and the idiosyncracies of his political environment. Within these constraints he may shape his role—and coax others to accept it. But he is always mindful of the surrounding conditions.

Part of these conditions are the political and administrative structures which function within the subsystem. Structure here, refers to continuing relationships or patterns of interdependence between individuals working on common tasks. In political structures, these tasks are primarily concerned with policy decisions. Some examples of these are: municipal councils, legislative committees, and party caucuses.

In contrast, administrative structures are preoccupied with techniques for implementing policy decisions. Because of this, they usually germinate within the bureaucracy and much of their time is taken up with coordination, either within an agency or between different bureaus grappling with common problems.

The brute facts of life however, rarely conform to neat categories and the boundaries between policy and administration are, in varying degrees, elusive. In fact, the impact that political and administrative structures have on each other is an important condition for urban decentralization. Where participants have a clear conception of their roles and are able to fulfill them, that impact will be mutually beneficial. Administrators and policy makers each strive toward that fulfillment, prodding one another from their different positions. Oftentimes boundaries are violated, but the action moves back and forth until the overall objective is achieved, modified, or abandoned. What occurs in this situation is a series of alternating responses between members of different structures. Each participant projects himself from that role upon a specific objective.

The reverse of this situation may also develop. Multiple structures may duplicate each others functions and relationships can easily strain. When interaction does take place, it is likely to be ridden with jealousy and harrassment. Members of political and administrative structures may be given responsibilities with incomplete means to carry them out, thereby keeping roles from being fulfilled. Rivalry between similar structures over scarce resources may further aggravate relationships.

Roles may also remain vague between members of rival structures. As a result participants will carry out their work in isolation and mix roles indiscriminantly; often to the point of confusion and counterproduction. Actors, in this case, lack clear conceptions about objectives, or guidelines on how to pursue them. Cooperation becomes rare and petty fights over the exercise of discretion erupt more frequently.

None of these conditions alone is likely to bring a subsystem to chaos. Danger comes when these conditions become cumulative and generate spinoff problems. Duplicating structures, rivalry between structures for scarce resources and attention, role ambiguity and their incomplete fulfillment; all rebound upon one another and permeate a subsystem with failure.

The nature of political and administrative structures also depends upon the internal coherence of the structures themselves. Established divisions of labor, clear perceptions of working roles, flexibility, and a firm rapport between all members contributes to organizational strength. That strength is vital when other parts of a subsystem begin to sag. The ability of a particular structure to assume additional burdens when legitimacy is weak or leadership falters, can make the difference between maintaining the dynamic of the subsystem or having it lapse into stalemate.

Weaknesses elsewhere may be rendered minor or made inconspicuous, because a political or administrative structure is able to compensate for them. Much as poor conditions can cause spinoffs which are deleterious, so too can coherent working structures magnify the vitality of a subsystem. In the following pages we will examine why some decentralized areas have been able to rely on and build on these strengths while others have not.

II. SUBSYSTEM LEGITIMACY

THE ROOTS OF LEGITIMACY

We have described subsystem legitimacy as the degree to which each of the decentralized areas was accorded acceptance and recognition. The circumstances behind the initiation of decentralization can have an important effect on how well a subsystem fares in getting its own constituency as well as various officials to recognize and support it. New York City's experience with decentralization illustrates how a highly personalized context of antagonism can surround that legitimacy with doubt.

A number of approaches to decentralization were undertaken in New York City in the mid-sixties; all of which were tied to the Mayoralty of John Lindsay. Among these was an attempt to establish a system of "little city halls" throughout the city. When members of the City Council rebuffed the plan, on grounds that the Mayor was attempting to build his own political machine in the neighborhoods, Lindsay resorted to private funds to get five "little city halls" located in trouble spots of the city.

Later the Lindsay administration took the lead in partitioning the city into sixty-two planning districts with their own Community Planning Boards. This was little more than an effort to recognize that identifiable communities did indeed exist within New York and provide each of them with an advisory planning unit. Also set up, within designated areas, were Neighborhood Action Programs (NAP's) which had some funds for capital improvement projects within their own communities.

The first serious effort devolving power to the city's neighborhoods was in the school system. This occurred in 1968, when three demonstration school districts were granted a measure of "community control." Community control turned into a sour experience for the Lindsay administration. New York City's teachers struck the schools over the issue and forced the Mayor into an ignominious retreat, resulting ultimately in the abolition of the demonstration districts.[3]

Through his second term of office, Lindsay came under increasing criticism from Governor Rockefeller. In his annual message before the state legislature, Rockefeller openly attacked Lindsay and argued that despite the concentration of power enjoyed by City Hall, the city was in a state of uncontrolled deterioration. The Governor urged greater local participation within the city itself—or loosely put, "decentralization" (The New York Times, Jan. 19, 1972: 39).

The seeming contradiction that two leaders could be at odds with one another about something that both ostensibly favored, like decentralization, is explicable by the different meaning each gave the term. For the Mayor, decentralization was a way of reaching into urban neighborhoods—or as some claimed, establishing Mayoral presence at the local level. For the Governor, decentralization was a method for breaking up inefficient concentrations of power—especially John Lindsay's power.

In any event, Rockefeller proceeded to secure his remedy by appointing a State Study Commission to investigate the city. Lindsay, in turn, reciprocated the favor by creating another commission to investigate the state. But there was too much public criticism for the Mayor not to feel the heat of demands for municipal reorganization.

Much of this came from the highly fragmented and competitive leadership of the Mayor's own Democratic Party within the city. Several of the Borough Presidents were expressing support for decentralization and proposals were published from their offices. While these plans used "neighborhood government" as a theme to spearhead reorganization, the plans projected the Borough Presidents as the new loci of power in the city.[4]

Meanwhile the State Study Commission had established an offshoot task force to hold public hearings and submit plans for restructuring the city's government. The task force was chaired by a former Democratic leader and frequent critic of Mayor Lindsay, Edward Costikyan. When in March of 1972, the task force made its recommendations public (Costikyan and Lehman, 1972), Lindsay angrily denounced them as "amateurish" and the work of a "Tammany politician" (The New York Times, Jan. 23, 1972: 39).

By the early part of 1972, the political circumstances behind reorganization seemed compelling; Lindsay had made a series of incomplete or unsuccessful starts toward greater community participation in the mid-

and late-sixties. Vestiges of these experiments still existed in half mori-bund form, and served as reminders of past failures. Political competitors within the city were threatening some kind of action on behalf of their own plans, which would have resurrected the borough presidents against the mayor's own power. The customary struggle between Mayor and Governor (or variations of it as, city v. suburb, upstate v. downstate, Democrats v. Republicans) had burst into open political warfare, but-tressed by a personal bitterness between Lindsay and Rockefeller. Finally, recommendations coming from the State Study Commission and its sep-arate task force forboded some action toward reorganizing power with the city.

The Lindsay administration's reaction to all of this was to argue that the proposals being made were "warmed over stuff" that had been con-sidered before and rejected. The administration also contended that com-munity participation had been tried earlier and was not feasible until administrative decentralization could first be made to work. In effect, Lindsay was shrewdly claiming that he was far ahead of anything being put forward and was attempting to hold the initiative on the issue.

The Mayor was able to strengthen his case with substantive action as well. At a press conference in December of 1971, Lindsay announced the introduction of several pilot projects in administrative decentralization. The projects were funded by a federal grant and were begun in the four communities observed for this study. The focus of these districts was to integrate services as well as encourage administrative decentralization of agency operations.

No formal provisions were made for community participation, though in all of the districts local citizen units of some kind (NAP's, Community Planning Boards or anti-poverty corporations) were still operating. Formal community participation, or what some considered political decentral-ization, was to be incorporated during a later phase of the subject. The rationale for this decision was to determine what the bureaucracy could produce after it was decentralized, before allowing citizen input. Lindsay had been hurt before in the school decentralization dispute and this was a way of embracing reform against the initiative of his critics, without incurring the risks of community participation.

In contrast to New York City, London's reorganization had markedly different roots. As in New York, reorganization was a controversial issue. But unlike in New York, those battles which occurred were fought within organizational, and not personal, contexts. The struggle for reform in London was a struggle to move London in a particular direction—whatever one might think of that direction—not an effort at personal entrepreneurship. The distinction, we think, is important because depersonalized innovation is more quickly able to become institutionalized, thereby endowing the new subsystem with legitimacy much sooner.

For Londoners great reforms never came lightly, nor without elaborate scrutiny and political debate.[5] Until the Greater London Act of 1963, the last major reoranization occurred in 1899, when the London County Council (LCC) was created. The LCC was an amalgamation of urbanized areas surrounding the ancient "City" of London and consisted of twenty-eight metropolitan boroughs plus The City. For the most part London's affairs were managed by County Hall, the official headquarters of the LCC.

Not until 1957 were there meaningful rumblings toward changing the London County Council. Spurred on by several White Papers on the subject a Royal Commission was formed to examine local government in and around London and make possible recommendations for change. The Herbert Commission, as the Royal body was known, was a nonpartisan group of business, professionals, academics and distinguished civil servants. For nearly three years the Commission held hearings and solicited testimony before issuing its final report in 1960, which was the basis for the Greater London Act. This essentially nonpartisan report was supported by a Conservative-sponsored document which came in the form of a Government White Paper.

With the inception of the Herbert Report and the Government's basic endorsement of its findings, the lines for and against reorganization grew sharper. On the one side favoring reform were: the Conservative Government of Harold Macmillan; the Conservative Party in Parliament; the London Municipal Society, which was a Conservative pressure group; a coalition of second tier local governments, which stood to gain power from reorganization; and a team of scholars from LSE which had provided the Herbert Commission with important testimony on behalf of reform. On the other side opposing reform were: the minority Labour Party, the London County Council, which stood to have portions of their domain incorporated into a Greater London; and a host of occupational interests (mainly doctors and teachers) which felt threatened by reorganization (Smallwood, 1965).

The struggle over reorganization was intense and the political stakes high, but the actual battles were institutional, structural and organizational in nature—not personal. The Labour Party opposed reorganization because it controlled the LCC and most of London's twenty-eight boroughs as well. Reorganization meant for them that the old LCC boundaries would be extended to encompass the more conservative suburbs, swallowing up

Socialist inner London in a sea of Toryism. The Conservatives publicly adopted more pristine motives for wanting to reorganize London, such as greater efficiency and the reinvigoration of local government.

The political losses and gains were equally apparent for different tiers of local government. For some of the first-tier county councils which were suburbs of London, there was a possible loss of territory or autonomy—or both—to a Greater London authority. For many-second tier units the Greater London Act promised additional powers to those areas which were to become new metropolitan boroughs (Smallwood, 1965). All of this was compounded by considerations as to what political party would benefit by the new electoral constituencies, and alignments were not always that neat, but the ingredient of organizational division remained paramount.

Indeed, a catalogue of the actors in the New York and London experiences reveals some interesting contrasts between the two cases. In New York, the main protagonists were Governor Rockefeller and Mayor Lindsay. In London, no individuals loom nearly as large. Sir Keith Joseph, for the Conservatives, and Lord Herbert Morrison, for Labour, were important spokesmen, but by no means linked to the merits and liabilities of the plan.

In New York a task force which set out to examine and make proposals on restructuring the city was chaired by a man whom the Mayor perceived as an arch political enemy and the antithesis of the reformist movement Lindsay was trying to represent. The Herbert Commission could hardly claim such color, and if anything its members were criticized for lack of political experience.

Even in the politically laden sphere of inter-governmental relations, there were significant differences. Those Borough Presidents in New York who submitted decentralization plans did so as individual political initiators, applying pressure to other competitors. Thus the position of a borough was represented as that taken by its president. In the London case, local units were represented as Essex, Kent, Surrey, or whatever council happened to be expressing itself on the matter. It was the institution of the local unit, and its interests which determined its position, not its foremost official.

Perhaps the most significant difference between the two cities was in the ultimate act of ratification. In New York, reorganization was accomplished through an executive order by Mayor Lindsay. London's reorganization was brought about by an act of Parliament. This act provided London's subsystems with a special status given it by a prestigious institution. New York subsystems could be perceived as transient and attached to the political fortunes of its Mayor—a man whose longevity was in doubt.

Because of their statutory underpinning London's boroughs could be viewed as durable realignments of power and administrative responsibility. Although this was less true among ordinary citizens,[7] perceptions of urban change were sharp in the minds of governing elites. In effect an edict had come down from the central government that a particular reordering of relationships was to take place and borough councillors, local administrators and the national civil service were mindful of what these changes entailed.

This realignment established an elaborate scheme of separate and concurrent powers between the Greater London Council (GLC) and the boroughs themselves. More important, the overall arrangements provided something which was rare for a large city: the giving of smaller localities within London a virtual monopoly of power within their own territories when it came to particular kinds of functions. The impact of this was considerable on the recognition and acceptance a subsystem could command.

LEGITIMIZATION IN PROCESS

Legitmacy is not something derived from statute and given by one institution to another. It must grow and be earned by those seeking it. Legitimacy then, can be thought of as a process by which acceptance and recognition are gained over a period of time and there are certain factors which determine how well a subsystem will be able to do this. We suggest that these measures of legitimacy consist of:

(1) the degree to which a subsystem holds a monopoly of power and administrative authority within its own area, or its monopoly status;

(2) the ability of a subsystem to convert its status and resources into a continuing form of public acceptance; and

(3) the image and symbols a subsystem can employ for developing an ongoing recognition.

The first condition, monopoly status, was absent in the New York City experiment. In none of the community districts did the decentralized operations enjoy attention as the sole or major neighborhood agency. Essentially, the projects were established under a central Office of Neighborhood Government (ONG) located near City Hall, with local ONG offices, as the decentralized operations were called, within the community districts they served. Thus there were Offices of Neighborhood Government in Crown Heights (ONG-CH), Bushwick (ONG-B), Wakefield Eden-wald (ONG-WE), and Washington Heights (ONG-WH).

In all of the community districts however, neighborhood units established under earlier Lindsay initiative continued to function and in many cases compete with the ONG projects. In Crown Heights and Washington Heights, Neighborhood Action Programs (NAP's) went about their business as usual. In Bushwick, an anti-poverty corporation also remained active. Community Planning Boards existed in all districts.

It is hardly surprising therefore that local ONG's were viewed as intruders in each of these areas, though the responses differed somewhat. In Bushwick, the community anti-poverty corporation was apprehensive and saw ONG-B as a threat to its own preeminence in that neighborhood. Wakefield-Edenwald was not so much a case of jealous resistence as an unwillingness to get involved with the new project. There, the Community Planning Board largely ignored ONG-WE. In both Crown Heights and Washington Heights attentions were divided between a local triumvirate consisting of a NAP, a Community Planning Board, and neighborhood government.

In all of the community districts a multiplicity of competing units provided a high potential for conflict. Where leaders controlled more than one of these units, as in Crown Heights, that conflict could be kept within tolerable bounds. At other times it remained below the surface, keeping relationships stilted and distant. In Washington Heights jealousies erupted into antagonism and even sabotage. Despite this danger, little or no precautions were taken to either dismantle competitive units or work out adjustments between them before neighborhood government was underway.

In the London situation, monopoly status was of course affirmed for the boroughs by parliamentary statute. London's boroughs are autonomous and, according to Smallwood (1965: 25), the single dispensing agents when it comes to such matters as: housing, personal health welfare, childrens services, inspection standards, local roads, borough planning and a variety of other services. All of this gives them a foothold with which to magnify their legitimacy.

The legitimacy is projected through the formation of the London Boroughs Association (LBA). The LBA consists of representatives from each of the boroughs and has appropriately been described as a "defense organization" intended to protect borough interests. In recent years it has provided a number of technical services and training schools, which have enabled the boroughs to stand on their own as governing entities. It has also vigorously lobbied against the building of motorways through some boroughs, and on behalf of borough interests concerning the transfer of parks and public housing from the GLC to the boroughs.

The upshot of this has been to buttress the legitimacy and monopoly status of the boroughs with a spirit of independence. This is most often expressed vis-à-vis the GLC, but its psychological impact on what local government considers to be its "rights" and "responsibilities" is significant. The mere fact that neighborhood government can conceive of protecting its autonomy in certain spheres and "represents" itself is something Londoners take for granted but New Yorkers cannot.[8]

The initial differences in monopoly status between the decentralized areas in the two cities portends another distinction, which brings us to the second condition: the conversion of status and resources into a continuing form of public acceptance. In the London boroughs of Tower Hamlets, Islington and Wandsworth, local acceptance flows from the borough's institutional capacity—that is, from the capacity of each of these boroughs to absorb grievances and act upon them. New York's ONG's are in no such position.

Some examples of the subsystems at work point up the consequences for their legitimacy. London boroughs are able to gain public acceptance with relative ease because each borough possesses an elected council to make policy, and full time administrators to carry it through. Demands for more public housing or improved recreational facilities can be brought before a borough council, embodied as legislation, and administered by a professional staff. Thus, each time residents of the borough have a problem resolved, that resolution takes place through the machinery of local government and acceptance of borough authority is likely to increase.

By contrast, New York's decentralized areas stressed administrative decentralization as a first step toward any real decentralization in policy-making. But this arrangement posed inordinate problems for the local ONG's. If the projects restricted themselves to merely improving coordination between different agencies (traffic and parks or drug prevention and police), then how could neighborhood government demonstrate that it could make a meaningful impact on the community it served? Administrative reorganization by itself has very little salience for the public; without public salience the impact of neighborhood government could hardly be felt, much less accepted as paving the way for political decentralization.

These problems were difficult enough, without the local ONG's also having other neighborhood units to contend with for community attention. In an effort to attract recognition, each ONG undertook a number of community improvement programs. In Bushwick a campaign to reduce deaths from lead paint poisoning was begun. In Washington Heights special efforts were started to deal with the problem of narcotics addiction among the youth. Crown Heights resorted to a number of approaches for dealing with traffic congestion. Even these modest programs were difficult to launch; Crown Heights, for example, achieved the dubious distinction of having taken eight months to get a yellow line painted alongside a sidewalk curb so that teachers in a nearby school could park their automobiles.

To compensate for these handicaps, District Managers made efforts to solicit direct support from groups in their communities. These efforts amounted to appearing before neighborhood civic, political and ethnic organizations to publicize and inform the groups about neighborhood government. At other times more elaborate efforts were made to formally communicate with community groups and seek out their ideas. Each of these were attempts to establish closer relationships with residents, and they were of some use. But they appeared flimsy compared to the use London boroughs could make of their institutions.

One of these institutions, the political party, plays an important socializing role at the borough level. In Tower Hamlets, Islington and Wandsworth, for example, the Labour Party publishes a manifesto prior to election time. This publication deals with local matters and enables the party to advertise its objectives and achievements for the community. Another device for gaining recognition is the "political surgery," which is conducted once every two weeks in Tower Hamlets and at regular intervals in the other two boroughs. A "political surgery" is a British version of clubhouse politics, where party leaders meet with local residents to offer a helping hand or perform favors of a minor nature. Unlike the attempts to build rapport in New York, the manifestos and "surgeries" derive from ordinary functions connected with local governance. Rarely are they overt attempts at politicking for the sake of recognition alone. More often, they are combined with the resolution of problems and need not bear the onus of political campaigns—though they are that in a subtle and continuing form.

Finally, the image and symbols a subsystem can employ for developing an ongoing recognition is important for building legitimacy. These devices are vital for establishing the presence of neighborhood government and fostering an identification between a new subsystem and its constituents.

While the seven subsystems in both New York and London were formed with a concern for community identifications, there were attendant problems. New Yorkers did not have experience with community government and the neighborhood was fast becoming an abstraction with its tangible elements disappearing. In London, most of the new boroughs were created by combining older ones and there was a problem of forging a singular identity. Tower Hamlets was formed out of three separate identities (Bethnal Green, Poplar, and Stepney); Islington out of two older boroughs (Finsbury and Islington); and similarly with Wandsworth which incorporated Battersea and Wandsworth.

Each of these boroughs, however, was able to approach its task with a considerable arsenal at its disposal. All three boroughs have public relations units which publish an assortment of yearbooks and brochures and issue press releases. Public relations officers also meet with visitors to the borough and represent it to the citizenry at large. In characteristic fashion the boroughs have also mixed public relations with ordinary functions. A number of citizen's advice centers operate under the aegis of the local Town Hall or receive funding from it. These centers help citizens on anything from consumer problems to welfare assistance or the perennial landlord-tenant squabble; thereby linking the role of local government to the life of the citizen.

Most of New York's ONG's, at the outset, did not have headquarters in their community districts. Instead, they operated out of makeshift office space, located in downtown Manhattan. The facilities eventually provided were storefront headquarters. No special offices were established to deal with the problem of public relations, so that each District Manager had to devote much of his own time toward building community recognition.

The most active ONG's in this regard were Crown Heights and Wakefield. In Wakefield-Edenwald the District Manager embarked upon what he called a "road-show"; the watchword being "no invitation to a community group is to be turned down." In addition to these ad hoc contacts more formalized communication with residents was made possible through a Community Advisory Board. This board consisted of leaders of local organizations who advised the district cabinet on youth programs. In Crown Heights the District Manager helped organize a "cultural festival" and neighborhood "workshops"; all of which helped promote ONG-CH.

In the other two ONG units there were some minor efforts made toward establishing recognition, but little of an ongoing nature. Most of the community districts in New York did not even have local news media through which to project some common sense of identity.

In sum, most of what has been done in New York's ONG's has been sporadic with only scattered instances of continuing programs to build recognition. Moreover there has been little connection between efforts to win community support and the "output" of the ONG's themselves. Some partial exceptions to this can be found in Crown Heights and Wakefield-Edenwald, but it remains an open question whether these local ONG's can develop and utilize their capacity to meet community expectations.

III. LEADERSHIP CAPABILITY

LEADERSHIP IN SEVEN SUBSYSTEMS

Previously we described leadership capability as the effectiveness with which top policy or administrative officials are able to guide a particular subsystem. Much of this effectiveness, we mentioned, depends upon the availability of formal sanctions and inducements to a subsystem's leadership.

In New York City, District Managers are the sole agents responsible for the performance of local ONG's. All other top administrators are drawn from various agencies within the city's vast bureaucracy. As head of an ONG unit, the District Manager has few "hard" powers he can apply to bring about the decentralization of services. He lacks budgetary powers over service representatives and is not able to manage, assign or promote their personnel.

The precarious arrangement of establishing district managers without managerial power was consistent with the theory behind neighborhood government. The theory prescribed that local ONG's were not so much to carry through decentralization themselves, as serve as a conduit through which decentralization could be achieved. To this end, district managers are to encourage cooperation across bureaucratic agencies and provide a framework so that service heads can respond to community needs and work together. Some of the service heads themselves undertake managerial and assignment tasks of bureaucratic personnel within the community district.

District Managers do however, occupy an official capacity as an extension of the Mayor's authority. As such they can make use of "soft" powers which include: chairing "cabinet meeting" of service representative, setting an agenda for each cabinet meeting, and making the most of their position as a common respository for information and communications within the neighborhood. This strategic positioning coupled with a skillful application of ideas, management, and persuasion can go a long way for an innovative district manager.

Leadership in London's boroughs is more complex. The British, as a rule, attempt to draw a sharp distinction between policy and administration. Leadership, therefore, is a two-pronged affair between the Party Leader, who presumably takes charge of all policy matters, and the Town Clerk-Chief Executive, who is responsible for administration.

Ideally, matters of policy are decided upon by elected representatives sitting as members of a borough's council or on its numerous committees.

In fact, most important policy decisions are decided in party caucus and ratified at formal legislative sessions. Leadership on policy matters then, often devolves upon elites within the majority party, particularly the Party Leader.

In each of the three boroughs observed, the actual power of a Party Leader varied according to a number of conditions which are discussed below. Formally speaking, a party leader's capability is not much greater than those of the District Manager's in New York. As chairman of the party's caucus he is a key figure in determining priorities, and is at the hub of the communications flow within his own party. Much like a District Manager, a Party Leader can build on these advantages and become a dominant voice within his borough.

On the administrative side, the Town Clerk-Chief Executive heads the bureaucratic arm of borough government. Formally, his role on policy is advisory and limited to presenting technical information to political leaders. Often though, information and advice slip into advocacy and an experienced Town Clerk can frequently sway important decisions. Indeed, a competent Town Clerk will be relied upon as a political tactician by party leaders.

As Chief Executive, the Town Clerk also exercises a certain amount of control over the administrative machinery of the borough. Unlike New York's District Manager, he is directly responsible for the bureaucracy's efficient management, its coordination and its organization. Thus, an able Chief Executive who is careful enough to avoid getting buried in bureaucratic minutae, yet wily enough to keep track of his administration, can play a decisive part in the life of his borough. Moreover, his position amidst the local bureaucracy gives him ample opportunity to filter information and policy choices up through the political apparatus.

THE DOMINANT LEADERSHIP MODEL

All of these observations concern the formal roles and powers of leaders in our seven subsystems. In reality leadership varies with three conditions which are:

(1) the socio-political characteristics of the decentralized areas;

(2) the extent to which elite cohesion can be brought about; and

(3) the personal abilities of leaders themselves.

Taking these variables into account, Tower Hamlets in London, and Crown Heights and Wakefield-Edenwald in New York, show a configuration of leadership which is highly concentrated and which we call a dominant leadership model. In this model, leadership is lodged at the top of the subsystem and flows downward. Thus, in Tower Hamlets, power flows from the Party Leader and Town Clerk-Chief Executive; in Crown Heights and Wakefield-Edenwald, the District Manager is the dominant actor within the subsystem.

The reasons for this are as important as the fact itself. As pointed out earlier, Tower Hamlets is the poorest of London's boroughs and has a strong working class tradition. Labour has always been the majority party within the borough and currently all of the borough's councillors are from that Party. The local Labour Party itself is extraordinarily uniform in ideological outlook and shuns any form of resistance to the law—even where the archenemy Tory is concerned.

A recent controversy over a Central Government measure to raise rents (the Housing and Finance Act) reflects these deferential attitudes. While Wandsworth and Islington were threatening noncompliance and demanding that the increases be slashed in half, Tower Hamlets voted to implement the Act, provided the Government make a token compromise. As one borough official related in an interview, "We had to take some reduction back to our people. So we asked the Ministry if they could do something for us, and they did." Tower Hamlets, one of the neediest of London's boroughs, was finally granted a reduction amounting to a few pence per week, which it gratefully accepted.

Such deference also spills over into community attitudes. While citizen activism is not unknown in Tower Hamlets, the borough is politically passive, and voting turnout is one of the lowest in London (Greater London Council, 1971: 84-97). This allows elite groups to control much of the borough's political life and increases the likelihood of cohesion within key policy structures of the borough. At the core of this cohesion is a leadership group which operates within the Labour Party and consists of Leader, Deputy Leader, Whip. and committee chairmen. The group also sits as the Policy Committee of the Borough Council where it formally acts out its role in establishing priorities for the subsystem.

Though nominally consisting of independent actors, relationships within the leadership group are hierarchical, with the Party Leader occupying the top of the pyramid. Elites are kept in tow by the considerable discretion exercised by the Leader. He not only selects his immediate aides—Deputy Leader, Whip, etc.—but also chooses chairmen of all legislative committees. Moreover, potential competitors are kept off balance by the dependent nature of their assignments. The Deputy Leader and Whip occupy their positions indefinitely, but may be removed at any time by the Leader. Committee chairmen rotate their offices annually and this prevents them from forming an independent base of power.

Even with these very substantial powers over his colleagues, the Leader within Tower Hamlets cannot act arbitrarily. All appointments are ultimately ratified by Party Caucus and a Leader can always be removed. Still, the Leader is a major source of political rewards and penalties within the borough. So long as he holds the confidence of other politicians, all political roads will terminate at his office and policy-making will crystallize at the top of the pyramid.

This crystallization of power is reflected in the administrative process as well. There, the Town Clerk-Chief Executive sits at the head of an administrative structure, known as the Management Team. This team consists of the Directors of the borough's major service divisions—Finance (accounting and revenue), Technical (planning, architecture, public works, etc.), Community Services (health, housing management, libraries, etc.) and Social Services (welfare, care for the elderly, etc.). Through this administrative structure all administrative reports are cleared and revised by the Chief Executive before reaching policy makers. While the management team affords a Chief Executive the opportunity to control his staff, it does not guarantee that control; much of this depends on a Chief Executive's personal abilities and the nature of his interaction with the Party's elites, particularly the Party Leader.

As a working-class borough which participated in the struggle for social legislation, Tower Hamlets has a tradition of "strong" leaders and its Town Clerk is no exception. In interviews with local party leaders and politicians within the borough, the talk is respectful of the Clerk's higher education and such comments as "he's second to none in all of London, maybe all of England" are not uncommon. One party influential readily admits that the Chief Executive "won't take any guff from anybody, when it comes to seeing his job through." Still another spoke of how the Clerk advises them in negotiating with the central ministries and added, "and what he tells us, you can be sure is right."

While the personal ability of a Chief Executive may strengthen his office, he must build on that office through other men at Town Hall. The crux of dominant leadership, therefore, lies in a constant interaction between the borough's Chief Executive and its equivalent of a machine "boss," the Party Leader. This interaction takes place on a regular basis when both men get together to discuss problems confronting the borough and strategies for dealing with them. The meetings are usually informal and revolve around the most pressing concerns: additional public housing, rental increases for tenants, industrial development and planning.

Both men are careful to keep abreast of their own staffs and exchange information with one another at these sessions. The meetings also enable them to set the direction of issues subsequently brought before two of the borough's major structures—the Policy Committee and the Management Team. When asked how important this prior consultation was in deciding issues, one leader responded, "Well, I'd feel as if I'd failed if we didn't sort matters out in advance and didn't know opinions before we went into a policy meeting."

This guidance, which emanates from a remote corner of Town Hall, is made part of the policy meetings of which the leader spoke. Policy meetings within the borough are held by a larger group of political elites and attended by the Management Team, which furnishes technical advice. At the meetings the Party Leader and Chief Executive move into their respective roles as head of one or the other structure and guide the deliberations, by fixing priorities and resolving differences within their own staffs. The overall effect is to form a nexus of power between the two leaders both before and during formal decision-making. Such an arrangement enables them to continue their influence over issues long after matters have left their desks.

Tower Hamlets then, presents a unique case which closely conforms to our model because all of its underlying conditions work to reinforce a dominant leadership style. The social and attitudinal climates within the borough are highly supportive; its leaders exercise an interlocking control over two major structures; both leaders are able men who have experience within the borough; and, close relationships between the leaders enable them to trade on one another's power so that firm control is assured.

While these conditions do not operate in as strongly a reinforcing direction in New York, there are strong similarities. Both Crown Heights and Wakefield-Edenwald are in working class neighborhoods, where residents are concerned about neighborhood deterioration and anxious to avoid its continuation. As a result the communities are supportive, and some groups enthusiastic, about ONG's presence in the neighborhood.[9]

In Crown Heights, the District Manager had prior experience working within that area. Before the inception of ONG-CH, he functioned as head of the local NAP unit and when neighborhood government began in Crown Heights, he found himself in the enviable position of heading both agencies. The dual role has enabled him to establish interlocking control over two major structures within that community. By capitalizing on the resources of both offices he has overcome many of the hazards which beset leaders in other subsystems and has parlayed these initial advantages into an innovative role for himself.

While other District Managers were struggling to obtain office space, ONG-CH availed itself of existing NAP facilities and the two units became indistinguishable. Early in ONG's history, conferences and open meetings were being conducted in Crown Heights, all of which were manned and organized by NAP employees. Block associations were encouraged to organize in an effort to stimulate community pride and homeownership. These activities were used to pinpoint neighborhood concerns (police and consumer protection, environment, recreation, education, etc.) and convince citizens of ONG's willingness to do something about these issues. The approach also succeeded in introducing the District Manager to civic groups throughout the area and helped sensitize local bureaucrats to citizen problems.

Drawing the bureaucracy closer to the community is, of course, a major objective of neighborhood government, but one which is more easily talked about than attainable. In Crown Heights the task was easier because service representatives had been working together as an administrative structure under NAP. When neighborhood government began there, service representatives simply reconstituted themselves, in modified form, as an ONG cabinet. While the District Manager lacked the authority of command, he could exploit cordial relationships which had developed under NAP and use them for newer goals. Thus when less experienced ONG leaders were still probing administrative structures for areas of cooperation, Crown Heights was already underway.

One of the techniques used to encourage new ventures between agencies is to organize task forces around problems of a major concern. Since the service cabinet within Crown Heights is quite large, the task force is a useful device for reducing the cabinet to small, manageable groups. It also enables the District Manager to emphasize service areas where his relationships are strongest, such as police and sanitation. Through the task force the District Manager meets with service heads and hammers out details of problems relating to a select number of agencies. The larger cabinet meetings, which take place monthly, are a sequel to and review of these smaller, informal operations.

A similiar technique used to organize interested parties around a common problem is one which the District Manager himself terms "ad hoc opportunism." This is a way to cope with bureaucratic ridigities by identifying crisis points within the community and applying pressure to outside agencies which can directly resolve a local grievance. The District Manager serves as a catalyst for community groups which are beset by a specific problem and assists them in finding a solution. In the past this has involved block associations to promote urban renewal, educational groups to organize school health fairs, and tenant groups to deal with broken sewer lines. This technique is a highly fluid one which defies neat organizational lines, but it has proven itself as a way for the District Manager to establish himself as an effective leader within the community.

Wakefield-Edenwald has a smaller cabinet, consisting of nine service heads, and its District Manager does not rely on task forces. Nevertheless, he exercises effective leadership for much the same reasons as does his counterpart in Crown Heights. Close, often informal, contacts are the rule between the nine service heads and the District Manager. Private meetings are sometimes held between selected administrators to work out particular plans, but the service cabinet is the mainstay of decentralization in that community. The cabinet meetings resemble informal conferences rather than the prearranged "report" formats popular with cabinets in other districts. At these seminar-type meetings information is actively solicited and problems identified for discussion. Strategies for problem resolution are also carefully worked out, and, as in Crown Heights, problems are often resolved by coordinating functions between different services. A high crime rate in a local park is handled by coordinating patrol activities between the representatives of police and parks. Improving methods for sweeping streets is arranged through cooperative action between highway and sanitation forces. All this takes place with the District Manager at the helm, steering service chiefs toward a meeting of the minds at these sessions, so that cooperative action can take place in the field.

The District Manager, by personal nature, seems eminently well suited for this intimate and direct arena. His extensive experience in both federal and municipal bureaucracies has provided the community with exceptional managerial talent. Wakefield-Edenwald is one of the few districts where modern management methods are consciously applied and where program planning is used to keep track of bureaucratic progress.

Fortunately enough, the District Manager's administrative sophistication is coupled with an earthy mannerism which is distinctly working class and which harmonizes well with his predominantly blue collar colleagues. Rapport between all members of the cabinet is excellent, with the District Manager regarded as part of a friendly clique rather than an alien imposed by City Hall.

Much like his counterpart in Crown Heights, the District Manager in Wakefield-Edenwald has also established himself as a source to which community groups can turn for help. During the first six months of his office, he meticulously rode circuit through all parts of Wakefield-Edenwald, visiting more than 80 organizations. This worked successfully to identify community problems and establish relationships with civic leaders. The not-so-accidental byproduct of these visits was to cultivate popular support for neighborhood government as well.

While the techniques of leadership are somewhat different in the two subsystems the operative rule is the same; before anything is undertaken, both leaders carefully hammer out a consensus among leaders in each of their administrative structures and build personal links between themselves and community group leaders. Leadership in New York then, depends on District Managers carving out areas of interaction between themselves and select groups of elites, which can be accomplished in several ways—task forces of administrators, interlocking control of structures, negotiations with civic leaders, and a personal style which engenders the confidence of one's colleagues.

In Crown Heights this has meant a fluid, sometimes ad hoc, pattern of relationships. Within the cabinet, the task force is the principle device by which these relationships are forged; it reduces an unwieldy body to manageable proportion, limits participation to areas where it can be exploited most fruitfully, and enables the District Manager to borrow more easily on his role as head of NAP. An extension of the task force concept is also used to motivate community groups toward action and assert the leadership of the District Manager.

In Wakefield-Edenwald, fruitful interrelationships have come about with the cabinet as a whole because of its manageable size, though spheres of personal interaction are also relied upon. Like Crown Heights, relationships with civic leaders are strong.

In London, elite interaction is also very much the key to strong leadership. Though there are significant institutional differences between London's boroughs and New York's community districts, there are also significant parallels which go deeply to the core of urban innovation. To be sure, leadership in Tower Hamlets is highly structured compared to that of Crown Heights and Wakefield-Edenwald. The British attempt to institutionalize the distinction between policy and admnistration through a hierarchical committee system and sharp divisions of labor. In spite of this, formal distinctions are quite often breached.

Common to all three subsystems is the reliance on private, informal contacts among elites, before decision-making ever occurs.[10] The success of these contacts depends on the personal abilities of the leader, his access to other resources, and his facility in trading on other men's powers.

A further aspect of leadership is that it involves a process of continual coalition-building. A distinguishing feature of the dominant leadership model, is that coalition-building originates with top leaders of a subsystem, who set broad goals and then negotiate a consensus around these goals with other elites. As this consensus grows and spreads downward throughout the subsystem, decision-making becomes increasingly formalized.

For example, in Tower Hamlets formalization begins when decisions move from the private conversations of Party Leader and Town Clerk to policy meetings, where specific courses of action are decided upon by political and administrative elites. The process matures as decisions wend their way through the local governing apparatus. In Crown Heights and Wakefield-Edenwald task forces and seminar-type meetings between service chiefs are used to develop this initial interaction. Formalization occurs as decisions are brought before monthly cabinet meetings or operationalized by service chiefs and foremen as they are carried through the bureaucracy.

Finally, some comment is in order regarding the relative effectiveness of dominant leadership in the London and New York subsystems. Regardless of its purely administrative intent, successful leadership requires skillful politicking. In London, leadership operated more smoothly because both leaders had sanctions and inducements to apply as a tool in coalition building. Londoners also recognize the political realities of decentralized governance and have incorporated strong local parties into their decentralized areas. This allows for a good deal of formalized political "input" through borough councils, party caucuses, and the like. Thus any consumer of services (tenants, welfare recipients, etc.) with a grievance might pay a visit to the Town Clerk-Chief Executive or address himself to party leaders and seek redress. This form of input not only allows leaders to frame larger issues on behalf of their constituents, but also socializes citizens into the political process and earns their support when critical problems arise.

By contrast, the New York projects never took political realities into account. Even where dominant leadership was possible, it was a very thorny affair. District Managers have fewer powers to apply against bureaucratic chiefs than do London's Town Clerks. Coalition building is therefore almost entirely a persuasive task with little a District Manager can offer to his service chiefs in exchange for their cooperation. This is why personality and style are more important in Crown Heights and Wakefield-Edenwald than they are in Tower Hamlets. Indeed, in Wakefield-Edenwald, dominant leadership is more the result of the District Manager's personal style, than of institutional factors. Where there are few institutional factors available to strengthen a leader's hand, the hazards of relying on individual performance are all the more increased.

The importance of personal ability in the New York situation is readily seen in the different emphasis District Managers gave to building political support in their areas. Shrewd leaders in Crown Heights and Wakefield-Edenwald cultivated political support among civic groups, while others did not or were unable to devote their attention to community groups. But even where this kind of interest aggregation was undertaken it was unstructured and carried out at the crude level of "community conferences" or "workships." The Mayor's office persisted in believing that the initial phase of decentralization could be carried out without a political component, and this contributed to the erratic performance of the ONG's.

DIFFUSE LEADERSHIP

Only three of our seven subsystems fall into a model of dominant leadership. The remaining four reveal varying degrees of diffuse leadership. Essentially, diffuse leadership is a pattern of authority which does not flow from one or two top leaders, but which emanates from a variety of elites and leaders of a subsystem. This model can be treated along a continuum where leadership becomes increasingly pluralistic or diffuse. Figure I locates each of the subsystems along this continuum, ranging from dominant leadership to low, medium, and high categories of diffuse leadership.

Whether leadership is of a low, medium, or high diffuse nature depends upon the conditions we mentioned earlier in analyzing leadership. Thus, where socio-political characteristics, elite cohesion, and the personal abilities of leaders work in a supportive direction and reinforce one another toward strong leadership (e.g., highly able leaders plus a cohesive political

FIGURE I

LEADERSHIP IN SEVEN SUBSYSTEMS

	Dominant Leadership	Low Diffuse	Medium Diffuse	High Diffuse
MODEL				
SUBSYSTEM	Tower Hamlets Crown Heights Wakefield – Edenwald	Wandsworth	Islington Washington-Heights	Bushwick

elite), a subsystem will be less diffuse in its leadership. On the other hand, when these conditions are nonsupportive of strong leadership or pull in contrary directions (e.g., highly able leaders but a factionalized political elite), a more diffuse pattern will emerge.

Wandsworth, for instance, is represented as a subsystem with low diffuse leadership; which means that only one side of the borough's two pronged leadership works in a consistently dominant pattern, while the other is fragmented. Like Tower Hamlets, Wandsworth's Town Clerk-Chief Executive and his Deputy are experienced men who take a firm hand in the borough's administration. However, the borough's political leadership is split between a traditional labor wing and a more radical Fabian's socialist faction. The upshot is a one sided, often spotty pattern of leadership.

While on the administrative side, The Management Team is steered by the Chief Executive, in-fighting often erupts between political elites. Vacillating party members often drift toward a radical course, only to be checked by traditional elements. This has weakened policy meetings, so that the party no longer functions as an instrument of consensus and direction.

As in Tower Hamlets, the controversy over the Housing and Finance Act in Wandsworth reflects the political character of the borough. The Council's Housing Committee, which had a radical majority, decided against implementation of the Act and recommended a policy of resistance to the law. A heated debate ensued within the Party Caucus. By a margin of one vote the Caucus voted to reverse the Housing Committee and with that vote, the existing political leadership was overturned. The Party Leader was replaced as were his aides and many committee chairmen. The radically dominated Housing Committee was offset by temporarily merging it with a committee dominated by traditionalists so that a new recommendation in favor of compliance could be made.

The Chief Executive has maneuvered deftly within this political setting to play an unusually influential role. During the Housing and Finance debates, he interceded with stern warnings about the illegality of resistance. On another occasion, he sent a tactfully worded letter to every elected member, enumerating the penalties the Government could impose on members who voted to defy the act.

Despite this assertive role, there are strong proscriptions against administrators overtly engaging in policy matters, and politicians are acutely sensitive to it. As one political leader said in an interview, "There is a haunting fear by many Members that they will be governed by Chief Officers. I think that is exaggerated but somewhat true."

If the Chief Executive in Wandsworth is to be effective then, he must be flexible and circumspect. A fragmented political structure necessitates that he maneuver within a changing political hierarchy and work with scattered pieces of authority (committee chairmen, party leaders and influential politicians). While Wandsworth is by no means directionless, its top leadership does not interlock and it is far more erratic and unsure of itself than Tower Hamlets.

Islington and Washington Heights are represented in Figure I as sub-systems with medium diffuse leadership. That is, with leadership which is exercised by multiple elites within middle rungs of the subsystem. By contrast to Wandsworth, neither of Islington's governing arms exert a consistently dominant leadership. Its Town Clerk-Chief Executive came into office under a compromise when the two boroughs of Finsbury and Islington were merged and he has never been able to work from a position of strength. Under the compromise, administrative power was split be-tween each of two older boroughs' leading administrators. Moreover, the new Chief Executive was appointed for an interim term, until his retire-ment came about. As a lame duck Chief Executive, he was handicapped in bringing a newly enlarged bureaucracy under his control. Others within the borough have pointed out that the Chief Executive added to these woes by immersing himself in detail only to lose sight of larger goals.

On the political side, Islington bears some resemblance to Wandsworth. Its Labour party is split between older working class traditionalists and younger middle class radicals, often referred to as Fabians or "leftist intellectuals." The latter group is made up of highly articulate profes-sionals (university lecturers, journalists, architects, etc.) who have recently moved into the borough and taken an active part in its political life.

After borough-wide elections in 1971, when Labour regained control of Islington, an internal struggle for power ensued between the two groups. The left wing of the Party successfully elected its candidate for Leader; an uneasy truce prevails today, with members of the old guard in several key positions. Furthermore, an already simmering citizen activism has been fueled by disputes over the Housing and Finance Act, which directly touches the pocketbooks of local residents. During borough debates over the Act, tenant groups and marginal political parties descended upon Town Hall, and citizens are steadily growing accustomed to direct political action.

Obviously these developments preclude closed pyramidal-type struc-tures of the kind that function in Tower Hamlets. Islington's Labour Leader has adjusted to these changes by shifting to a mediating rather than a command role, and he has done this proficiently. While the leader must be active, he is no longer the source of the borough's political direction. Instead, he works to bring various influentials together or to facilitate their requests.

Unlike Tower Hamlets, where direction emanates from an interlocking administrative and political leadership, or Wandsworth where a concentrated administrative leadership interacts with a diffuse political elite; power in Islington flows along horizontal rather than vertical lines. Usually this means that committee chairmen must work closely with second or third rung administrative officers from a particular service. Policy meetings within the borough have withered as a source of leadership strength and one politician derisively refers to them as "the dustbins of the Council."[11] Instead, decisions tend to focus within particular committee structures, with interested actors clustering around middle rungs of power. Leadership is also diffuse in Washington Heights and more so in Bushwick. While Crown Heights has been able to mitigate its problems of multiple structures and an unwieldly cabinet, the District Manager in Washington Heights has met with no such fortune. Within Washington Heights the Community Board and NAP not only have separate leaders, but each of these leaders enjoys an independent base of power. The Community Board, for instance, is one of the most active in the city and is in the rare position of having a small paid staff. The Borough President of Manhattan has also seen fit to delegate some autonomy to Community Boards and this has contributed to the zest with which its leader guards its prerogatives. It has some control over leases granted to municipal agencies in the area and managed to prevent neighborhood government from obtaining office space in Washington Heights for nearly eight months. Washington Heights' NAP enjoys a similar stature. The Community Board's leader is a prominent member of the community and has contacts with citizen's groups and political clubs within the area.

This split in power is itself a formidable barrier to the exercise of dominant leadership by ONG-WH. In addition, City Hall chose not to consult with neighborhood groups in selecting the District Manager, which gave credence to the suspicion that an agent of the Mayor was being imposed on the community. In subsequent months the District Manager became embroiled in negotiations to resolve these misunderstandings. The negotiations succeeded only in diverting ONG-WH from its immediate priorities and debilitated the entire project. During the first five months only two cabinet meetings were held and even there, relationships were strained. On one occasion, a cabinet representative failed to appear and instead sent his deputy, who left midway through the meeting. The District Manager reacted by sending off a strong protest, which served only to heighten tensions. Task forces were also begun within the service cabinet, but with little success.

Some observers (Higinbotham and Boyle, 1973: 47-ff) claim that ONG-WH's troubles were exacerbated by a District Manager whose experience was exclusively in formal positions of command and management. According to this interpretation, the District Manager was unable to cope with his new role which was informal and required patience and leadership by example rather than by order. It appears more likely that a series of disadvantageous conditions rebounded upon one another to split leadership in Washington Heights. With no powers or incentives to bring these three leaders together, it will continue to remain diffuse.

Of all the subsystems, Bushwick has the most fragmented leadership structure. Social conditions are so dismal that leaders perceive the situation as hopeless and are not inclined toward vigorous action. While this attitude is inexcusable, it is not difficult to appreciate its basis. A survey of housing in the area led to a recommendation that any serious attempt at inspection would mean the condemnation of nearly all of the area's residences.

Leadership behavior tends to be apathetic and solitary. While leaders are able to complete routine tasks, they work in isolation from one another, and there seems to be little the District Manager is able to do about it. Poor coterminality between service districts in Bushwick has swelled its cabinet to more than 20 members. Despite this, little has been done to reduce it to manageable levels so that strong leadership can emerge. More often than not, bureaucrats are off on their own assignments with little opportunity for interaction.

Apparently, diffuse leadership has taken some toll on the ability of New York's subsystems to implement or complete community programs. Of the four neighborhood governments, Bushwick is at the bottom with only 21% of its programs successfully undertaken; Washington Heights is third with a 54% success rate; while Wakefield-Edenwald is second with 56%; and Crown Heights at the top with 81% (Adler, 1973).

IV. STRUCTURAL CAPABILITY

THE CONCEPT AND IMPLICATIONS OF STRUCTURAL CAPABILITY

Thus far we have looked at different models of leadership in New York City and London. In this final section we will examine more closely the substance of those elite relationships by using the concept of structural capability. Structural capability refers to the effectiveness with which political and administrative structures interact with one another in undertaking their tasks. The more effective this interaction, we claim, the more cooperative elite relationships will be in carrying out particular tasks.

It will be recalled that Tower Hamlets, Crown Heights and Wakefield-Edenwald were analyzed as dominant leadership subsystems. In each of these decentralized areas the application of leadership at the top was sufficient to bring a complex of working relationships about. Also in the model, strong leadership was the key factor and depended on highly skillful administrators using a variety of devices to build coalitions.

What happens then when leadership begins to fragment, and what can we learn about the structural capability of a subsystem when diffusion occurs? Some useful comparisons can be made, if we analyze a variety of diffuse models, ranging from a low diffusion in Wandsworth which progressively increases in Islington, Washington Heights and Bushwick.

In each of these diffuse subsystems, effectiveness depends not so much on the presence or absence of a strong personality, but on something intrinsic to the system itself, which is apart from the strength or weakness of a particular individual. Structural conditions appear to channel the energies of actors toward functional or dysfunctional ends. Regardless of personality, where political or administrative structures are successfully able to mesh with one another, tight cooperative relationships ensue between elites. When these structures are unable to relate to one another in a mutually productive way, elites split apart, in lethargic indifference or bitter acrimony. The nature of this interaction and the reasons for it are essential for understanding the successes and failures of urban innovation. Hence we can add to our earlier models of leadership a new dimension, called elite interaction. This dimension reflects the substance of elite relationships and may be combined with our four leadership models as Figure II below indicates.

In the dominant leadership models, strong direction was exerted from the top to forge tight relationships among leaders and elites. In Tower Hamlets and Crown Heights, concentrated and multiple sources of power shaped these relationships—hence their interlocking nature. In Wakefield-Edenwald the District Manager had no interlocking powers, but relied on personal style and goodwill to establish cooperative relationships, which were centered around his office.

When leadership begins to collapse into low, medium and diffuse models, some intriguing patterns emerge in the nature of elite interaction. New York subsystems fall into a competing or noncooperating pattern of interaction, whereas those in London remain cooperative. This, we claim,

FIGURE II

LEADERSHIP MODELS AND THE NATURE OF ELITE INTERACTION

Models of Leadership

	Dominant Leadership	Low Diffuse	Medium Diffuse	High Diffuse
Inter- locking Elites	Tower Hamlet Crown Heights			
Cooperat- ing Elites	Wakefield- Edenwald	Wandsworth	Islington	
Competing Elites			Washington Heights	
Non Coop- erating Elites				Bushwick

is attributable to the structural differences between the subsystems. For the remainder of this section we will examine these differences and the internal dynamics which stem from them.

COMPETITION AND NONCOOPERATION IN NEW YORK

Washington Heights and Bushwick are respectively characterized as subsystems with competing and noncooperating elites. In each case, competition or noncooperation can be traced to the structural capabilities—or noncapabilities—of the two areas. In Washington Heights elite interaction is structured so that not only do overlapping tasks cause a great deal of confusion, but these arrangements also breed a destructive rivalry over scarce resources and prestige. Bushwick presents a rather different problem which is not uncommon for blighted areas in American cities. It suffers from nonaction, which is insulated by a lack of accountability within the subsystem.

From the very start of neighborhood government in New York City ONG-WH had its problems with multiple structures competing with it for local legitimacy. This alone was a serious problem, but one which was exacerbated by the fact that the local NAP and Community Planning Board also had claims to many of the same functions that neighborhood government was supposed to undertake. The Community Planning Board saw itself as both the object and source of local opinion and had functioned in that role for some time prior to the ONG experiment. Its purposes were highly political and its leader formed a convenient alliance with the local NAP, which was largely an administrative structure. This alliance worked well, so long as the two structures divided the labor and complemented one another. Happily for the members of both structures, the Community Board listened to and interpreted public opinion concerning planning and development, while NAP had also played a hand in funding and administering capital projects. The leader of NAP had also begun to work with a service cabinet of agency representatives in an attempt to coordinate the bureaucracy around select projects.

All this was bound to change when the Mayor's new approach to neighborhood government came to Washington Heights. City Hall assumed that after an initial period of adjustment, the District Manager for ONG-WH would work himself into this relationship and form a harmonious triumverate.

City Hall quickly learned that the ways of politics and bureaucracy are not easily tampered with, when it comes to neighborhood power. Neighborhood government in Washington Heights not only faced obstacles in getting office space, but was circumscribed in its political contracts. Organizations and political clubs in the community, which had been accustomed to dealing with either the Community Board or NAP, were chary of working with still a third structure, which for them made little sense. In reaction, the District Manager pushed on with independent projects, first maneuvering to gain control over NAP and then attempting to slip away from being held accountable to the Community Board.

Organizational problems were soon translated into personal quarrels and as the situation worsened the District Manager (Middleton, 1972) finally appealed to the City Hall, writing:

> In the absence of an internal reorganization plan which would finally clarify the relationships between . . . the District Manager and the Washington Heights NAP, I can expect continuing confusion and complications from both agencies and from community organizations. Such confusion has led several agency and community representatives to yet another unnecessary level of city bureaucracy. While initially I felt that the existence of an independent and distinct NAP office in my district would have complemented and

supplemented my efforts, it has become increasingly clear to me that this goal is not practical.

Further on the District Manager pointed up the suspicions which made cooperation so difficult in the area:

> The major complication that this lack of definition . . . has created is a gross misunderstanding on the part of the Chairman of the Community Planning Board as to the nature and responsibilities of the District Manager. More than that, it would appear that the Chairman of the Community Planning Board and several other very influential community leaders have . . . come to view the role of the District Manager as basically undermining . . . both the NAP and the Community Planning Board. I feel that . . . priority attention must be paid to this . . . dilemma if the full potential of service integration and command decentralization is to be realized.

Earlier, City Hall chose to evade the issue, hoping somehow that leaders would be able to negotiate what was left unsaid. This time, with the problem perched at its doorstep, the central administration had little choice. It responded in typical form, first supporting the District Manager in principle, only to hinder him in working out the details of a modus vivendi.

In defense of ONG-WH, City Hall refused to bow to political pressure that it be dismantled and stood firm on the continuance of neighborhood government in that area. On the other hand, its solution for the dispute was to incorporate both the Community Board and NAP into the operations of ONG-WH. The heads of each structure were given the power of advice and consent in ONG's decision-making. The Community Board reserved this prerogative for "projects and procedures involving policy decisions" (i.e., political questions involving choice); while NAP held this priviledge in matters relating to "the operations of government" (i.e., administrative concerns). Over the objections of the District Manager, the Community Board was also given a seat on his cabinet, and it was further stipulated that both the Community Board and NAP "shall be the channels through which the District Manager coordinates community contacts" (Office of Neighborhood Government, 1972).

After the Mayor's staff finished defending neighborhood government in Washington Heights, it was difficult to appreciate what was left of it. Somewhere in the miasma of written agreements, the District Manager was designated as the "chief administrative coordinator of municipal government" in the area. But behind the ambiguous phraseology of "cooperation" and "full consultation," it was apparent what had been negotiated. ONG-WH had been squeezed between an administrative and political structure; neither of which would willingly give up their powers. Rather than force these structures to do so, City Hall took refuge behind vague pronouncements.

The conditions negotiated made it unlikely that functional relationships could be brought about between the contending leaders. In the first place, the agreements forced ONG-WH into an overlapping and conflicting role with the other two structures. If the Community Board was to continue in its political qua policy-making role, and NAP in its governmental and managerial capacity; then the District Manager's position would be made untenable. Any District Manager with enough gumption to see his job through had to be cast in some political role—merely if that entailed identifying local problems and establishing rapport with community organizations. Yet these tasks were also apportioned to the Community Board and, in some instances, to NAP.

Similarly, undertaking service improvement and community development put ONG's District Manager on a collision course with NAP, whose leader had been working with the service cabinet and who, under the agreement, would continue to play an active role in "the day to day operation of government." Whatever the District Manager did with respect to politics or administration he was faced with the Hobson's choice of running headlong into one or another community structure, or abandoning his own role.

Secondly, the conflicts which City Hall did not settle, were "resolved" by an advice and consent formula which allowed both NAP and the Community Board veto power within neighborhood government itself. Essentially, ONG-WH was encumbered by a system of checks against projects it wanted to undertake. The entire relationship was a negative one, based on the prevention of action, rather than positive accomplishment. It is hard to envision how such an arrangement could have produced anything but a tug of war between all three structures.

Third, the mood and reality of all government in New York City is one of scarcity and Washington Heights is no exception. Scarce resources, funds, and even public attention pervade the community. Local residents could hardly be expected to absorb three neighborhood units tripping over one another in quest of recognition, nor would central administrators be likely to tolerate this.

The outcome of these conditions has been to internalize tensions rather than release them toward productive ends. Projects are hampered because cabinet members are reluctant to become involved with a District Manager who has influential enemies in the community. These arrangements have apparently taken their toll on what ONG-WH has been able to accomplish. Next to Bushwick it has the lowest record of successful "output" of the four decentralized areas. Even minimal efforts to curb narcotics addiction and improve public safety have been unduly delayed and still face obstacles. All in all, a dysfunctional competition continues to damage community governance in Washington Heights.

The situation in Bushwick, although less administratively complex, is more serious than those of other decentralized areas. Rather than relationships which are dysfunctionally competitive, it suffers from an absence of interaction. While 70% of the population is black or Puerto Rican, its bureaucracy is overwhelmingly white (Higinbotham and Boyle, 1973: 8-16). Racial and ethnic polarization contributes to this indifference and is aggravated by the depressing poverty of the neighborhood. Residents are alienated by what they consider to be an alien and uncaring civil service. Officials complain of citizenry which does little to help itself and roughnecks who assault firemen and building inspectors. The natural reflex, under these conditions, is avoidance rather than cooperation—even competitive involvement is shunned.

Avoidance appears to characterize the working style of ONG-B itself. Bushwick has been the slowest of the neighborhood units in knitting its cabinet into a working body. During the first six months of the experiment, it had little direction and nothing was undertaken during that time. The District Manager, who is himself black, has had difficulty building a cohesive cabinet. Cabinet attendance has been poor and meetings are sometimes cancelled for lack of a quorum. At least two municipal agencies delayed assigning representatives to the cabinet and even when bureaucrats are assigned, they lack enough managerial authority to accomplish anything.

No doubt, the appalling social conditions of Bushwick weigh heavily on neighborhood government. However, structural deficiencies are also apparent. Its cabinet lacks any kind of accountability either between members, to the District Manager, or to community groups. Incentives for performance are noticeably absent and, could go far in improving municipal services. What Bushwick misses in structural capability, we contend, can be seen in two London subsystems which are analyzed below.

LONDON'S SUBSYSTEMS AND THE DYNAMIC OF ACCOUNTABILITY

Although Wandsworth and Islington have diffuse leadership, it should not be assumed that these subsystems are less effective than those which have dominant leadership. On the contrary, a strong argument can be made that diffuse leadership, because it is less hierarchical, is likely to be more flexible and creative in meeting problems. Normative arguments, as the value of democracy and citizen participation, might also be advanced for subsystems with multiple elites rather than those with concentrated leadership.

Aside from these concerns, the fact is that a decentralized area can be effective without dominant leadership if it has the structural capability to do so. What makes for this capability in London's subsystems can be summarized as (1) a formal division of roles between political and administrative structures coupled with interaction between these structures and (2) the presence of citizen input and accountability with these structures. These two conditions, we claim, contribute to a dynamic of interaction by which functional relationships are brought about.

The first of these conditions, formal division of roles, is one which political science has not emphasized in the past decade. Modern political scientists have instead emphasized elite behavior and attitudes as explanatory variables for political systems (Almond and Powell, 1966; Macridis, 1955). We believe behavioral factors are important, but would also stress the part that formal roles play in shaping that behavior. From our own observance of these subsystems at work, formal allocations of power act as important cueing devices and reference points from which actors project themselves. The allocation of these roles provides a starting point from which interaction can grow in a functional or dysfunctional direction.

In Wandsworth and Islington, the starting point is the distinction made between policy and administration. Elites within these subsystems identify with one or the other role and assume an identity and responsibility in accordance with it. This occurs throughout every rung of the subsystem, from the distinct roles of Party Leader and Town Clerk down through ordinary committee members working with lesser administrative deputies. Hierarchy is not always maintained and elites of different status may work together; as when committee members consult directly with a Town Clerk or with a Director of an encompassing service. Nor is perfect symmetry kept; so that not every administrative service has its exact committee counterpart. Nonetheless, both the administrative and political prongs of local government converge around every goal. Every issue has the attention of members of political and administrative structures approaching it via their different tasks.

On any given issue—be it the construction of borough housing, additional playgrounds, or free transportation for the elderly—broad policy decisions will be made in party caucus or by a particular committee. These decisions will be presented to administrative officers at the upper rungs of the bureaucracy to work out technical details or begin implementation.

From that point on, the refinements of policy and administration are carried out by committee or subcommittee members working jointly with a Chief Officer and other administrators. These relationships are premised on a formal division of roles between policy makers and administrators, and all actors begin their work from either of these two perspectives regardless of where in the borough hierarchy this interaction takes place. Policy makers concentrate on matters of desirability or choice, while administrators furnish "technical data" for impending decisions and report on the administration of ongoing policies.

Interaction of this kind is sometimes carried out in formal committee, where a version of the parliamentary question and answer period is relied upon to proceed with the business of the day. Politicians question bureaucrats on the status of new projects and praise or criticize them on the administration of others. Administrators often prepare for these sessions with lengthy reports or with elaborate data that comes with the invariable requests for information on housing costs, traffic congestion, disease rates, etc.

At other times, informal arrangements between politicians and bureaucrats are utilized. This may be limited to personal contacts between a committee member and an officer; or "working parties" may be used to coordinate the actions of a group of actors around a common problem.

Whatever the arrangement, roles are defined and structured so that collisions, though not always avoided, are minimized. Politicians are wary of aggressive administrators pushing their ideas into policy matters. Similarly, administrators are often frustrated over stubborn politicians, who refuse to yield to their advice. When conflicts become so dysfunctional that they threaten the goals themselves, one or the other can make a hasty retreat, using the formal definition of his role to guide his actions. When, in the last resort, there is no retreat, it is the policy maker as the elected representative of the borough, who reigns supreme. An example of this occurred in one borough when a newly elected Conservative majority decided to sell off public housing to private ownership. While the Tories believed housing could better be provided through private enterprise, administrators felt differently and advised against it. When their advice went unheeded the borough's officers delayed action on property assessments, hoping that Labor would regain control before drastic changes were made. Nevertheless Tory leadership persisted and in the end forced the professionals to comply with their policies. Administrators were able to salvage their prestige (and jobs as well) by falling back on their formal roles as "neutral" civil servants working to implement a political mandate.

More often than not, cooperation is the rule from the outset and each actor takes charge of his own responsibilities, while holding each other accountable. Administrators are expected to carry out decisions promptly and efficiently. Policy makers are obliged to render judgements on difficult questions and make decisions on further choices growing out of the implementation of past policies. Those tensions which occur between elites are goal-oriented, and derived from expectations about the completion of specific tasks. (This contrasts sharply with Washington Heights, where tensions are the result of role instability.) In short, the beginnings of mutual accountability based upon achievement and response are formed.

This interaction is buttressed by still another source of accountability from nongoverning actors which is built into the subsystem through citizen input and accountability. The traditional means for this has been for citizens to present petitions to Town Hall and have them formally considered by the borough council. More recently, the idea of citizen participation has gained increasing attention and is gradually being incorporated into Wandsworth and Islington in a variety of ways.

In both of these boroughs most committee and subcommittee meetings have been made public, and the press and citizenry are invited to attend. On controversial issues, hearing rooms are frequently packed and tickets must be alloted in advance on a first come basis. At these meetings, ordinary citizens join in on the question and answer sessions, formerly reserved for politicians and administrators. Comments and reports are made on the intricacies of rodent control, building repairs and care of mentally retarded children. Citizens appear as witnesses and give information where none was available before, or bring problems up to date through their testimony.

The upshot of this input has been to enhance accountability between political and administrative structures. While the division between political and administrative tasks is roughly maintained, still a third task—that of continued information input—is incorporated into the relationship. This has the advantage of putting forth fresh viewpoints from the consumer-citizen, without jeopardizing working relationships between these structures. The presence of "outsiders" at these meetings also serves as a mild and informal oversight on governing elites. Elites are sensitive to what the press reports and especially to what activist citizens are thinking.

The growing popularity of citizen involvement has initiated some devolution of authority within local bureaucracies and other kinds of direct participation. In Wandsworth and Islington, some service bureaus have been divided into territorial units, so that a "mini" decentralization of managerial authority can take place. Housing and social services are the prime targets for this kind of conversion. In some instances, administrative devolutions have been combined with formal citizen input. Wandsworth has four "District Housing Panels" plus a fifth borough-wide panel which oversees and advises on managerial problems. The panels consist of representatives from tenant associations and councillors, and have administrative officers at their regular meetings. Social services too, have been divided into smaller localities within the boroughs. Wandsworth has created five territorial subdivisions within its bureau of social services, while Islington has opted for still smaller units and established ten such subdivisions. The creation of smaller territorial divisions now provides the opportunity for structuring additional citizen input into these functions.

Of the three London boroughs, Islington holds the most promise for increased citizen participation. It alone has established a special advisory committee to investigate the question of citizen participation and consultation. In its *Report to the Policy Committee* (14, Dec. 1971), some recent proposals include: extending the formalizing citizen consultation into key committees; establishing an elaborate system of local forums which could deal separately with special-purpose problems and problems specific to a locality; building closer relationships with educational institutions; holding additional broad-purpose civic conferences; and publishing a borough newsletter. The notion of local forums to be held regularly within different wards of the borough is especially attractive to younger intellectuals, who are talking about the further devolution of government to populations of ten-thousand citizens. This would extend beyond mere consultation to some measure of administrative control. These proposals are still at the deliberative stage, but it seems likely that at least some changes will be adopted.

Citizen participation within Wandsworth and most especially Islington has had a momentum of its own—both in the process and substance of decision making. The more these boroughs have devolved power, the greater have been the demands from citizen groups. Increased demands when met, appear to generate additional mechanisms for citizen input, only to put still more pressures on the subsystem and create a spiraling cycle. Much of this pressure is also brought about by lower echelon administrators, like social workers, who are in daily contact with needy clients and help them lobby for additional benefits. Administrative decentralization has facilitated this, and close alliances between young civil servants and their clients are causing a radical transformation in the process of policy initiation in some areas.

Citizen input and activity can partially be seen in the funding appropriated to voluntary organization by their respective boroughs since reorganization began in 1965. The pattern of this funding, shown in Table I, serves as a useful measure for a borough's disposition to support interest groups as well as the group's ability to lobby on its own behalf for assistance.

VOLUNTARY ORGANIZATION & GRANTS IN AID FOR THREE LONDON BOROUGHS[a]

Borough	1965-66 No.	1965-66 Am't £	1966-67 No.	1966-67 Am't £	1967-68 No.	1967-68 Am't £	1968-69 No.	1968-69 Am't £	1969-70 No.	1969-70 Am't £	1970-71 No.	1970-71 Am't £	1971-72 No.	1971-72 Am't £
Tower Hamlets	37	49,175	44	48,903	56	51,710	59	54,111	58	59,131	69	113,586*	69	67,397
Wandsworth	24	---	34	61,175	40	65,826	32	66,419	32	78,459	34	69,198	44	93,659
Islington	25	59,500	28	67,020	31	63,660	33	69,870	33	75,440	34	72,980	41	120,730

a. Data are derived from budgetary sources and minutes of the policy committee in Tower Hamlets, Wandsworth and Islington.

* This figure includes grants for capital expenditures in the borough made during one year, and is not useful for our purposes.

As Table I indicates, Islington shows a consistent increase in both the number of citizen groups receiving borough monies and the total amounts given them. While the number of voluntary groups increased by over two thirds, total funding doubled. This dramatic increase reflects the political dynamics of that borough. As leadership becomes more diffuse, citizen participation reinforces the subsystem's structural capability. Groups became more active in the borough by contributing to the interaction between politicians and administrators and overseeing it. In recent years considerable pressure has been put on governing elites to make them accountable and citizen groups are increasingly able to exert pressure by means of a lateral entry into the subsystem (i.e., by devices which enable them to work with committee chairmen and chief officers)—or sometimes from the bottom up (i.e., appealing through petitions, local forums, etc.).

Wandsworth shows less dramatic increases, but ones which are still significant. While the total number of groups receiving funds increased by almost one third, appropriations for voluntary groups rose over fifty percent. This fits the pattern of increased participation at the lower levels. Earlier, we described Wandsworth as a low or partially diffuse subsystem and this may have a bearing on why voluntary group funding is lower in Wandsworth than it is in Islington.

Tower Hamlets is a contrasting picture to those of Wandsworth and Islington, though the data need greater explanation. While the total number of groups receiving assistance is the highest of all three boroughs, its total funding is the lowest with only a slight increase since reorganization. This is due to the fact that as a poor working class borough, Tower Hamlets contains an unusual number of charitable organizations, any of which date back to the "soup kitchens" of the 1920s. Still, there is a relatively low rate of funding for these groups because the borough's leadership is unwilling to give up its dominant role (or yield to what it considers to be "private paternalism"). Tower Hamlets is among the minority of London's boroughs which has done little to provide for direct citizen participation—or even allow for some kind of oversight. Its committee meetings remain closed to the press and the public, and its politicians are unusually chary of speaking to "outsiders."

To a remarkable degree then, those London boroughs which have deconcentrated power have adapted to it by strengthening their structural capability. As top leaders have lost their grip, other governing elites and citizens have obtained greater control. This control has been kept in tow by roles which are so defined as to channel energies away from personal power conflicts toward functional goals. Citizen accountability has also been structured into this interaction so that incentives are provided to maintain high levels of performance. A comparable diffusion of dominant leadership in Crown Heights or Wakefield-Edenwald, we hypothesize, would not engender the same adaptive response. New York's subsystems rely very heavily on the idiosyncracies of their leadership and so long as this is the case, we doubt that compensatory action can be generated should top leadership collapse.

Finally, something should be mentioned about the trend of popular participation in Wandsworth and Islington. Thus far, citizen participation has been functional for each of these subsystems. We would however be cautious about pushing this too fast and too far. If, as we suggest, increased participation also means increased demands, there could be a serious overload on the borough. Aside from the financial strain, governing elites may not be able to deliver on higher expectations. Already, some civil servants are openly complaining about inordinate workloads because of local activism. Some politicians fear that civil servants, and especially unions, will resist popular intrusion into their bailiwicks. If this materializes, there could be a rebellion in all the rungs of the borough hierarchy, which would upset the delicate balance upon which all interaction is built.

V. CONCLUSIONS

This study has concentrated on the relationships between conditions surrounding decentralization and decision making processes within decentralized subsystems. We have hypothesized that three conditions must be fulfilled if decentralization is to be successful. These conditions have been summarized as:

(1) subsystem legitimacy;
(2) leadership capability; and
(3) structural capability.

Our concern has been to present these conditions as necessary prerequisites for generating functional relationships between all participants in a subsystem. As such we have highlighted processes rather than policy outputs and we have used these outputs only to portray different kinds of relationships between top leaders, administrators, politicians, and citizen groups.

Our analysis suggests that when three conditions operate in a favorable direction interaction within a decentralized area will be enhanced and so will the chances for more successful innovation. Thus, if subsystem legitimacy is to be achieved for a newly decentralized area, monopoly status and public recognition should be maximized. The practical applications of this mean that local administrations should retain control over as many public activities as possible. Separate boards or councils for education, planning or health bring about destructive political competition and limits a new administration's ability to gain acceptance through its own policy outputs.

In addition we have argued that strengthening leadership capability requires that leaders have interlocking sources of control and tacit approval to carry out tasks which are "political." Without these requisites they can only be saddled with formal responsibilities without the tangible powers to carry them out.

Structural capability can also be strengthened by sharply defining roles between different levels of policy makers and administrators and by dilineating areas of interaction between them. A cautious encouragement of citizen participation into various aspects of decision making can also go a long way toward promoting better government by keeping elites alert and informed about emerging problems.

No doubt there are many able and talented leaders within the subsystems we have examined. Nevertheless, we found that ad hoc arrangements which are based solely on personal ties can be extremely limiting and are often fraught with hazards. Unless such relationships are also given permanent and formal status, innovation will be precarious. For without well defined and permanent relationships, participants will clash over their alleged responsibilities, as occurred in Washington Heights, or languish in confusion, as happened in Bushwick.

A primary goal of decentralization—be it administrative or political—is to provide a process which increases the scope of access in all aspects of decision making. While administrative decentralization seeks to accomplish this by involving more personnel in the management of municipal serives, political decentralization attempts to expand the citizen's role in matters of basic policy.

In New York the effort to embark solely upon the administrative aspects of decentralization could not be undertaken successfully. As a result, leaders were obliged to cultivate a political clientele. Interest groups were sought out for support and political leaders contacted. London experienced no such problems, because the framers of decentralization were, in our opinion, far more realistic.

In addition, we observed that when formal structures do not exist or roles are not clearly defined, participation can be badly distorted. While structures in London's scheme do not guarantee constituent or group participation they do provide the *opportunity* for such participation. The New York City experiment did not provide these channels but sought participation from the community in a haphazard fashion. Each districts' operating procedures differed and there were no generally recognized channels for input. Because of this, the nature and scope of the community's involvement depended upon how each leader defined his role and the roles of those with whom he interacted. As a result involvement was dominated by the most articulate and well organized groups in the community. Those groups with the most power and visibility were sought out while those with the least were virtually ignored. In effect, some of the New York's subsystems unwittingly gravitated toward an early closure of access and succeeded in opening the subsystem to one segment of the community but shut it off to another. This consequence, if continued, could violate the very basis of decentralization in that city, which is to introduce flexibility and broader perspective into the governing apparatus.

In the end the success of decentralization will depend upon its ability to cope with problems which confront mass society. Regardless of the many laudatory arguments made for greater democratization, streets must be cleaned and children must be well educated. Yet only recently have we learned that "experts" can be very limited in knowing what is best for the citizen/consumer and that the citizen himself cannot avoid crucial decisions. Only through the mounting nature of the "urban crisis" have we come to appreciate the necessity of checking the power of the professional so that he can better serve his clientele (Crozier, 1967). As one noted author comments "The potential for finding solutions can only be enhanced by the broader range of alternatives offered by laymen" (Gittell, 1972: 684). Decentralization can lead the way for that search if administrative and political institutions are designed to accommodate the wealth of perspectives which arise in urban communities.

NOTES

1. The term subsystem is used here to depict a microcosm of a larger system such as Greater London or New York City. System or subsystem is defined as "a persistent pattern of relationships involving power and authority which results in the allocation of values" (Farkas, 1971: 97-8).

2. The variations of population in London's boroughs are greater than New York's community districts. The London boroughs, for example, range from as little

as 140,000 to 300,000, while in New York the populations hover in the 150,000 range. Nevertheless in both cities politicians and administrators took great care in preserving community characteristics and making them co-terminous with the newly decentralized areas (Office of the Mayor, 1970; Greater London Council, 1970; Greater London Council, 1971).

3. However, a weakened form of local participation in school policy still exists. Local boards are now popularly elected but with fewer powers than those held by the original demonstration districts. For a history of this subject see Maurice Rerube and Marilyn Gittell (1970) and Martin Mayer (1968).

4. While the Borough Presidents' plans differed in detail the one overriding scheme was to establish neighborhood councils which were primarily responsible to the respective President of each borough. The obvious intent was to undercut the Mayor's power by isolating him from grass roots leadership at the community level and placing the Borough President in the position of intermediary between City Hall and smaller communities (Abrams, 1970; Sutton, 1972; Manes, 1972).

5. There are several excellent up-to-date treatments of London's reorganization. Each of these accounts stresses a different approach to the subjects with S. K. Ruck (1970) providing a brief but incisive overview of the reorganization; Smallwood (1965) using a conceptual and interest group approach, and Rhodes (1970) focusing on the historical development of the Greater London Act.

6. First-tier county councils were created by the Local Government Act of 1888. They were elected bodies designated to carry out the administration of county affairs. They were to act as the "primary local governmental authorities . . . delegating to their smaller 'second tier' units (Municipal Borough, Urban Districts, Rural Districts, Parish Councils) specific functions, to be administered on a more localized basis" (Smallwood, 1965: 63).

7. According to a public opinion survey conducted soon after London's reorganization, well over a majority of citizens knew what had taken place and could identify the initials of the GLC. Nevertheless one third of the citizenry were unable to do so (Greater London Council, 1966: 9).

8. The importance as well as the autonomy of London's boroughs is evident in some of the vital statistics concerning the boroughs and the Greater London Council (GLC). The total GLC staff numbers 120,000 while the boroughs employ a total of 227,000, nearly twice the GLC figure. The same relationship holds also for budget figures. In the area of housing, the boroughs own and manage over 400,000 permanent dwellings and the GLC half as much with 200,000 (Sayre, November 1971; Dawtry, May 1971; London Boroughs Association, 1972).

9. Many of these feelings were revealed in a series of community hearings conducted in each of New York's boroughs by the Charter Commission for New York City (Spring, 1972).

10. For the purpose of this essay the term "elite" refers to a combination of officials legally charged with political decisions and those policy and opinion leaders that influence the making of decisions.

11. This statement is exaggerated somewhat but relatively valid. Policy meetings in Islington are not as paramount a force as they are in Tower Hamlets, but still carry considerable weight and political elites are working harder to rebuild them as a source of strength.

REFERENCES

ABRAMS R. (1970) A Plan For Borough and Neighborhood Government in New York City. New York: Office of the Borough President of the Bronx (Mimeograph).

ADLER, M. W. (1973) "Project output in five experimental districts." New York: Urban Analysis Center, City Univ. of New York (Unpublished Report).

ALMOND, G. and G. B. POWELL, JR. (1966) Comparative Politics. Boston: Little, Brown.

ALTSHULER, A. (1970) Community Control. New York: Pegasus.

ARNSTEIN, S. (1969) "A leader of citizen participation." Journal of the American Institute of Planners 35 (July).

BERUBE, M. and M. GITTELL (1969) [eds.] Confrontation at Ocean Hill Brownsville. New York: Praeger.

BROWER, M. (1970) Why Do We Need Community Corporations For Ghetto Development. Cambridge: Center For Economic Development.

Charter Commission For New York City (1972) Public Hearings in Bronx County, New York. The State Study Commission for New York City, New York, N.Y.

COSTIKYAN, E. and M. LEHMAN (1972) Restructuring the Government of New York City, New York: The Task Force on Jurisdiction and Structure of the New York State Commission for Charter Revision.

CROZIER, M. (1967) The Bureaucratic Phenomenon. Chicago: Univ. of Chicago Press.

DAHL, R. (1961) WHO Governs. New Haven: Yale Univ. Press.

DAWTRY, A. (1971) "Reorganization of the government of London." London: (Paper Prepared National Conference of Cities).

EASTON, D. (1965) A Systems Analysis of Political Life. New York: John Wiley & Sons.

FANTINI, M., M. GITTELL, and R. MAGAT (1970) Community Control and the Urban School. New York: Praeger.

FARKAS, S. (1971) Urban Lobbying. New York: New York Univ. Press.

FELSER, J. W. (1965) "Approaches to the understanding of decentralization." Journal of Politics 27 (October): 536-566.

GITTELL, M. (1972) "Decentralization and citizen participation in education." Public Administration Rev. (Special Issue, October).

Greater London Council (1971) London Borough Elections of 13 May 1971, London: Greater London Council.

――― (1970) The Municipal Yearbook of 1970. London: Greater London Council.

HIGINBOTHAM, S. J. and J. M. BOYLE (1973) "Between community and city bureaucracy: New York's district manager experiment." New York: Bureau of Applied Social Research, Columbia Univ. (Unpublished Report).

KAUFMAN, H. (1969) "Administrative decentralization and political power." Public Administration Rev. 29 (January-February).

KOTLER, M. (1969) Neighborhood Government. Indianapolis: Bobbs-Merrill.

KRISTOL, I. (1968) "Decentralization for What?" Public Interest 11 (Spring): 17-25.

LIPSET, S. M. (1960) Political Man. New York: Doubleday.

LIPSKY, M. (1971) "Street Level bureaucracy and the analysis of urban reform." Urban Affairs Quarterly (June): 391-410.

London Borough of Islington (1971) Report to the Policy Committee, 14 Dec. (Mimeograph).

London Boroughs Association (1972) London Boroughs Handbook, London: London Boroughs Association.

MACRIDIS, R. (1955) Comparative Government. New York: Random House.

MANES, D. (1972) A Program for Restructuring New York City Government. Office of The Borough President of Queens.

MAYER, M. (1968) The Teacher's Strike. New York: Harper & Row.

MIDDLETON, D. J. (February 1972) "District manager's status report." New York (Unpublished Report).

MILLER, S. M. and M. REIN (1969) "Participation, poverty and administration." Public Administration Review (January-February): 15-25.

The New York Times (January 19, 1972, January 23, 1972).

NORDLINGER, E. A. (1972) Decentralizing the City: A Study of Boston's Little City Halls. Boston: The Boston Urban Observatory.

Office of the Mayor (1970) A Plan for Neighborhood Government for New York City. New York (Mimeograph).

Office of Neighborhood Government (April, 1972) "Proposed statement on working relationships between Community Board 12, the Executive Committee, the NAP, and the Office of Neighborhood Government." New York (Unpublished Report).

Public Information Service of the Greater London Council (1966) "Survey of Londoner's knowledge of the Council and its work." London: Greater London Council.

RHODES, G. (1970) The Government of London: The Struggle For Reform. Toronto: Univ. of Toronto Press.

ROSENBLOOM, R. and R. MARRIS (1969) [eds.] Cambridge: Social Innovation In The City. Cambridge: Harvard Univ. Press.

RUCK, S. K. (1970) The Government of Greater London. London: George Unwin Ltd.

SAYRE, W. (1971) "The relevance of the greater London government's experience to New York City government." New York (Mimeograph Prepared For The State Study Commission For New York City).

SCHMANDT, H. (1973) "Decentralization: A structural imperative." in H. G. Frederickson (ed.) Politics, Public Administration and Neighborhood Control. California: Chandler Publishing.

SMALLWOOD, F. (1965) Greater London: The Politics of Metropolitan Reform. New York: Bobbs-Merrill Co., Inc.

SUTTON, P. (1972) A Plan for Localized Government in New York City. New York: Office of the Borough President of Manhattan (Mimeograph).

U.S. Bureau of the Census (1970) Census of Population and Housing. Washington, D.C.: Government Printing Office.

H. V. SAVITCH has taught urban government at New York University and was the Director of the Institute for Urban Studies, Jersey City, N.J. He is currently an Associate Professor at SUNY, at Purchase. He has published articles in the fields of public policy and urban government and is currently doing research on mayoral leadership in American cities. He studied at Long Island, Brown and Michigan Universities and received his Ph.D. from New York University.

Professor Savitch has worked in the area of urban decentralization for a number of years, particularly in New York City. In 1972 and 1973, he traveled to London to work on the comparative aspects of this subject and examined how the London experience might apply to a major American city.

MADELEINE W. ADLER is an assistant professor of Political Science at Queens College, City University of New York. She is the director of the New York City Decentralization Studies funded by the Urban Analysis Center of CUNY. In addition, she is the author of "In Search of Decentralization" The Urban Advocate, Winter 1973, "A Selected Bibliography on Urban Decentralization," Urban Analysis Center, Spring 1973, and "Toward the Learning of Participatory Citizenship" with N. Adler and C. Harrington, Impact, Spring 1971.